KENTUCKY'S BOONE

The Pioneer Spirit

by

K. MELISSA BURTON

Illustrations by James Asher

International Standard Book Number 978-1-934898-03-1
Library of Congress Card Catalog Number 2008936926

Cover design and book layout by Asher Graphics
Illustrations/photography by James Asher
Photographs taken at Blue Licks Battlefield State Park and the Pioneer Museum,
Ft. Harrod State Park, Ft. Boonesborough State Park, Constitution Square State Park,
Kentucky's Capitol, and Cumberland Gap National Historic Park.

Manufactured in the United States of America

All book order correspondence should be addressed to:

McClanahan Publishing House, Inc.
P.o. Box 100
Kuttawa, KY 42055

270-388-9388
800-544-6959
270-388-6186 FAX

www.kybooks.com

INTRODUCTION

You've probably heard of the famous Kentucky **pioneer** Daniel Boone. Maybe you've even heard of other settlers such as James Harrod, Simon Kenton, or George Rogers Clark. But did you ever stop to think about the hundreds of other brave men, women, and children who left their homes and came to this wild land the American Indians called "Kain-tuck-ee"? Who were these people, and why did they come? What was life like when they got here?

Come along and find out, and as you read, ask yourself, "Could I have been a Kentucky pioneer?"

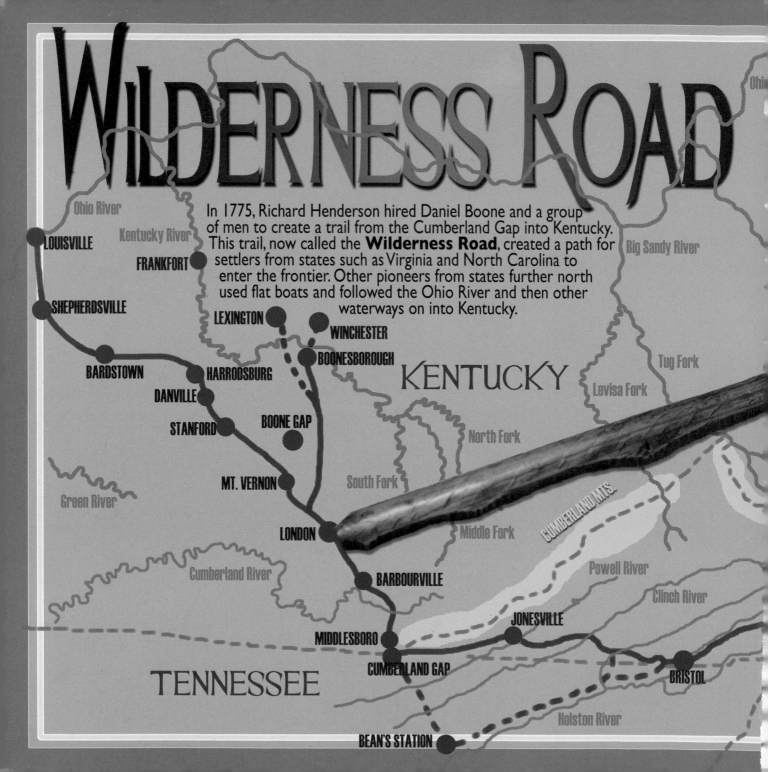

WILDERNESS ROAD

In 1775, Richard Henderson hired Daniel Boone and a group of men to create a trail from the Cumberland Gap into Kentucky. This trail, now called the **Wilderness Road**, created a path for settlers from states such as Virginia and North Carolina to enter the frontier. Other pioneers from states further north used flat boats and followed the Ohio River and then other waterways on into Kentucky.

Ohio River
Kentucky River
LOUISVILLE
FRANKFORT
SHEPHERDSVILLE
LEXINGTON
WINCHESTER
BARDSTOWN
HARRODSBURG
BOONESBOROUGH
DANVILLE
STANFORD
BOONE GAP
KENTUCKY
Big Sandy River
Tug Fork
Levisa Fork
North Fork
MT. VERNON
South Fork
Green River
LONDON
Middle Fork
CUMBERLAND MTS.
Powell River
Cumberland River
BARBOURVILLE
Clinch River
JONESVILLE
MIDDLESBORO
CUMBERLAND GAP
BRISTOL
TENNESSEE
Holston River
BEAN'S STATION

Their reasons for coming were as different as the people themselves. Some felt the east had grown too crowded and were hoping to purchase some inexpensive land. Others were starting new businesses. A few were simply adventurous. Whatever their purpose for coming, every settler came to the untamed land hoping for a better life.

But when they arrived, life was anything but easy.

WEST VIRGINIA

Tomahawks were used by both the Pioneers and the American Indians.

Allegheny Mts.

Shenandoah

SALEM

ROANOKE

INGLES FERRY

VIRGINIA

NORTH CAROLINA

NOW THAT'S INTERESTING

• In 1750, Thomas Walker led an organized expedition into Kentucky and was the first to record the existence of the Cumberland Gap on April 13th.

• Richard Henderson *thought* he bought the land of Kentucky from the Cherokee Indians. He wanted it to be named Transylvania and believed it would become the fourteenth colony.

• Boone and his men were attacked by American Indians shortly before finishing the trail. Three men were killed and some survivors turned back to Virginia.

• Between 1775-1810, about 300,000 people came through the Cumberland Gap.

• The Cumberland Gap is a natural **geographic feature** near the borders of Virginia, Tennessee, and Kentucky.

• The space between the mountains was made by an ancient creek.

• Often, the wood from a family's flatboat was used to build furniture for their new home.

• Kentucky's first settlement was established by James Harrod in 1774. The settlement is now the town of Harrodsburg. However, the first fort was built in 1775 at Boonesborough.

• There were about 250 forts and stations in Kentucky by 1799.

SURVIVAL ON THE FRONTIER

Living on the frontier took a great deal of hard work and energy. Without stores nearby and with many items being **scarce**, the pioneers had to use the area's **natural resources** to survive. Some of the resources Kentucky had to offer included fresh water supplies, abundant wildlife, fertile soil, and plenty of wood.

MAKING SOAP

MAKING CANDLES

NOW THAT'S INTERESTING

• Bear fat was used to make everyday candles. Beeswax candles were saved for special occasions because they did not smell.

Strings and ropes would be made from various plant fibers. Bast fibers, found in the bark of trees, would be used to make cordage and rope. Dogbang, a type of milkweed, could be used to make a very strong string.

If you were moving to a new home and could only take five items, what would they be?

BLACKSMITH SHOP

FOOD

Without the proper skills, starvation on the frontier was a real possibility. Hunting, growing, cooking, and preserving food took up most of any pioneer's time and energy. Often men would hunt in groups in hopes of bringing back a large game such as a deer or a bear. Other times, people of all ages would scout for berries, nuts, and herbs that grew naturally in the forest. With time, the pioneers were able to grow their own corn, squash, and beans. The Iroquois called this trio "The Three Sisters."

NOW THAT'S INTERESTING

• The pioneers often settled near natural salt licks so it would be available for the seasoning and curing of foods.

• Woodsmen would often take jerky, parched peas, and corn on their hunting trips. It was the original "fast food."

• No part of an animal was wasted. Whatever wasn't eaten would be used to make something else such as clothing or tools. Deer sinew (tendon) would be dried, pounded, and pulled apart and used as string to tie objects together.

• Simon Kenton was the first to plant corn north of the Kentucky River.

To keep food from spoiling, it was **cured**, or preserved, in other ways. Some foods, especially fruits and vegetables, were dried in the sun. They would then be rehydrated with water and cooked. Other foods such as meats and fish were either smoked or packed in salt to prevent harmful bacteria from forming. Whatever the method, if enough food was not preserved, it was certain to be a long, hungry winter.

Shelter

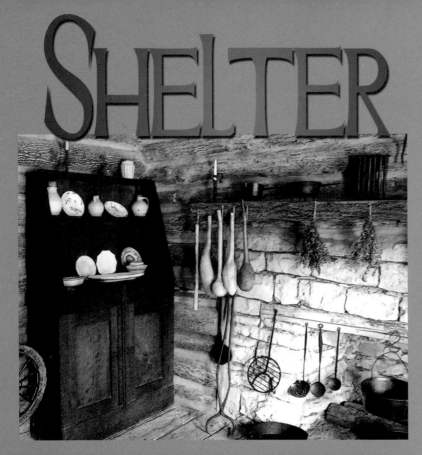

Now That's Interesting

• Poor drainage, animals, and dirty conditions made a fort a stinky place. New people often joked they could smell it before they could see it.

• The average family had 5 to 6 kids!

• The settlers took baths about once a week.

• Think about this: deodorant wasn't invented until 1911!

• All buildings and furniture had to be made with wooden pegs. There were no metal nails on the frontier!

• A carpenter was sometimes called "a joiner." Can you think of a reason why?

Dirt floor and straw bed   (right) Butter churn

Try to imagine your entire family living in a **shelter** about the size of your bedroom. Now try to imagine that room having only a dirt floor, one bed, no running water or electricity, and only a fireplace for light, heat, and cooking! When a family came to a fort, those were often the conditions.

In coming to the frontier, most families only brought weapons, ammunition, farming and carpentry tools, and a few pans for cooking. Other items would have to be made from the materials in the area. Furniture had to be built once families arrived, so often the children would end up sleeping together on a straw mattress in a loft or on the floor. You may not like the idea of sleeping with your brothers or sisters, but it was the best way to keep warm in the winter. Families lived this way until they could claim their land and build a place of their own.

Sleeping area has a rope bed and straw-filled mattress.

CLOTHING

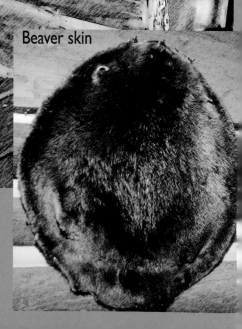

Beaver skin

- Ann McGinty brought the first spinning wheel to Kentucky at Fort Harrod.

- Flowers and nuts would be used to create dyes for fabric.

- Linen made from flax was also used in wrapping the mummies of ancient Egypt.

- Before flax could be grown, fibers in nettles were used to make cloth.

You probably know the pioneers used animal skins for clothing, shoes, and blankets. You probably also know that wool comes from sheep. But did you realize that Kentucky's earliest settlers didn't use wool at all? Instead, they made much of their cloth from a plant called flax.

Flax

Bringing a heard of sheep along the Wilderness Road or down a river was not practical, so when the early settlers arrived, they would plant a field of flax. This plant, when grown, can be then be harvested and run through a heckling comb. After it's been run through, the flax can be put on a spinning wheel and made into thread. Using a loom, the thread is then made into linen. The linen could then be used to make clothing, napkins, tablecloths, or other items.

At the Loom

PIONEER EDUCATION

Education had a very different meaning for pioneer children. Fort Harrod was the site of Kentucky's first schoolhouse, but it looked nothing like the schools of today. Children would sit on rough wooden benches and learn the alphabet by studying a wooden paddle where the letters had been carved. Students would go to school to learn the basics of reading, writing, and math.

However, for most children, these skills were taught at home, if they were taught at all. Many people of this time could not read or write. Instead, children were taught the skills they needed to manage a house, farm, and family. This makes sense in an environment where there were very few books and signs to read. Often, the only book available was the Bible.

At the age of fourteen, some children went to live with another person to learn a trade. When a child did this, he or she was said to be an **apprentice**. The apprentice lived with the master for seven years. The master provided food, shelter, and clothing for the apprentice while he or she learned the trade. At the end of seven years, the apprentice would be skilled enough to practice the trade on his own. Some would study to be a cobbler (shoe maker), carpenter, doctor, or blacksmith. What trade would you have chosen?

> ·1776· 1935
> TO THE MEMORY OF
> MRS. WILLIAM COOMES
> WHO HERE OPENED AND TAUGHT
> THE FIRST SCHOOL IN KENTUCKY
>
> PLACED BY
> THE KENTUCKY CHAPTER
> INTERNATIONAL FEDERATION OF
> CATHOLIC ALUMNAE

NOW THAT'S INTERESTING

• Jane Coomes from Maryland was Kentucky's first schoolteacher.

• Parents had to pay teachers. If money was not available, they would pay with chickens, deer, vegetables, or other goods.

CONFLICT ON THE FRONTIER

When the pioneer settlers came across the Appalachian Mountains, they were not the first group of people here. The Cherokee, Shawnee, and Chickasaw Indians were familiar with what is now Kentucky. Other tribes such as the Delaware, Iroquois, and the Miami also used the area as a valuable hunting ground. The "white men's" settlements, along with years of broken promises and a clash of cultures, created mistrust on both sides. The resulting conflicts were often deadly.

The start of the Revolutionary War only made tensions between the settlers and the American Indians worse. The British, knowing of the discord between the two parties, often encouraged the Indians to raid settlements. The raids struck fear into many of the pioneers who then returned back east. For a time, there was so much fighting that Kentucky earned the nickname the "Dark and Bloody Ground."

KIDNAPPING

In July 1776, Daniel Boone's daughter, Jemima, and two of her friends, Betsy and Fanny Callaway, were enjoying a canoe ride down the Kentucky River. When their canoe floated close to the bank, they were kidnapped by a group of Shawnee. The girls' screams alerted the fort and a search party was quickly formed. Three days later, while the Shawnee were cooking breakfast, Boone and a group of men ambushed the kidnappers and rescued the girls.

HARD TIMES AT FORT HARROD

Most settlers didn't recognize the treaty Richard Henderson made with the Cherokee as being legal. As a result, in 1776, a group of representatives selected George Rogers Clark and John Gabriel Jones to travel to Virginia and request the area of Kentucky become a part of the already established state. The request was granted, and Kentucky officially became Kentucky County, Virginia.

As part of the agreement, twenty-four year old George Rogers Clark was made a major in the Kentucky Militia and was granted 500 pounds of gunpowder to defend Kentucky's settlements against Indian attacks. Much of his military planning was done in one of the blockhouses at Fort Harrod.

George Rogers Clark's headquarters at Fort Harrod
Harrodsburg, Kentucky

In March of 1777, the area around Fort Harrod was attacked four times. Those living outside the fort rushed into it for protection. By the end of the month, everything outside the fort was ruined, including homes, crops, and livestock.

NOW THAT'S INTEERESTING

• Famous statesman Patrick Henry was the governor of Virginia when Kentucky was made one of its counties.

• Clark was the older brother of William Clark, one-half of the famous exploring duo Lewis and Clark.

• In 1809, Clark had a stroke and fell into a fire. His leg was burned so badly it had to be amputated.

THE GREAT SIEGE OF BOONESBOROUGH

In January 1778, Boone and a group of men were on a salt-making expedition near the Licking River. While hunting for food, Boone was overtaken by a group of Shawnee. To keep the Indians from attacking the unprepared fort, Boone surrendered himself and his men and convinced the Indians that the settlers would surrender the following spring. Boone and his men were taken as hostages. All but Boone were ransomed, and Boone eventually became the adopted son of Chief Blackfish. His Shawnee name was "Shel-to-y" which means "big turtle."

But in June, Boone overheard some men discussing an attack on Fort Boonesborough. Eventually, he was able to escape and traveled 160 miles over four days in order to warn the other settlers.

Boone was met with doubt. Some believed he'd become a traitor and was siding with the British and Indians. But in September, Boone was proven correct when the fort was attacked. Despite Chief Blackfish's attempts to negotiate with his adopted son, the citizens of the fort refused to surrender, even though they were outnumbered.

For the next several days, the Shawnee and British regulars attacked the settlement. Fire was used to try and burn it, and a tunnel was dug to make a way inside. Both efforts failed due to rain. By the end of the siege, it was clear the outmanned settlers had defeated their attackers.

NOW THAT'S INTERESTING

• During the siege, some women dressed as men and fired guns to make the Shawnee think more men were in the fort.

• Squire Boone, Daniel's brother, rigged a wooden cannon that was able to be used once or twice before it cracked.

• Squire also used old musket barrels to make something similar to the modern-day water gun. They were used to help put out any fires.

• In 1779, Chief Blackfish was shot in the leg when his village was attacked. He lived through the attack but later died from the infected wound.

• After the siege, Daniel Boone received a court-martial and was tried for treason. He was found not guilty, but left the fort soon thereafter and eventually settled in Boone's Station.

BATTLE OF BLUE LICKS

Even though British General Cornwallis surrendered at Yorktown in October 1781, fighting still continued in the frontier regions.

In August 1782, a band of British and Indians surrounded Bryan's Station in what is today Fayette County. Militia from neighboring forts and stations rushed to assist their fellow settlers. By the time they arrived, the enemy had already retreated. A Kentucky militia of 182 men followed them, which is what the British

and Indians had wanted all along. When the pioneer forces arrived at Blue Licks, they had walked right into an ambush. With 50 British soldiers (Canadian Rangers) and roughly 300 American Indians, the Kentuckians were grossly outnumbered. As a result, over 60 Kentuckians died, including Daniel Boone's son, Israel. It was a devastating defeat for the settlers and is considered by some scholars to be the "Last Battle of the Revolution."

Powderhorn believed to have survived the Battle of Blue Licks is on display at the Pioneer Museum at Blue Licks Battlefield. It belonged to battle survivor Robert Pogue.

FUN ON THE FRONTIER

Deer antlers would be cut and dots painted on the pieces in order to make dice.

Dolls were made of just about anything from corn cobs to bedposts.

• The game of jacks was originally called knucklebones. It was played with small pieces of animals bones that were roughly in the same shape as the jacks we know today.

While life was hard, even the pioneers managed to have some fun. Often, groups of people would get together for weddings and celebrations or to complete a big job such as corn husking, log rolling, or building a house or barn. These events would allow the settlers to get together and talk, exchange news, eat a good meal, and maybe even dance.

There were games as well. Foot races were popular as well as charades, jacks, marbles, and sometimes even tomahawk throwing!

Just as people of today enjoy a good tale, so did the early settlers. Storytelling helped to pass the time along the Wilderness Road.

TELLING TALL TALES ON THE TRAIL

Round stones and drilled pottery disks thought to have been used in games by American Indians are on display at the Pioneer Museum at the Blue Lick Battlefield.

PUT A FEATHER IN HIS HAT AND CALLED IT MACARONI

Yankee Doodle was originally a song sung by the British to poke fun at the colonists, whom they called "Yankees" and regarded as "country bumpkins." However, by the time of the Revolutionary War, the colonists were proud to be called Yankees and used the song as a rallying cry.

NOW THAT'S INTERESTING

• Yankee Doodle is the state song of Connecticut.

• Macaroni did not refer to small tubes of pasta. Instead, it was a very fancy style of dress popular in Italy and England.

Life on the Frontier

The pioneer diet depended on a number of factors. The earliest settlers were able to hunt wild game in the area, but did not have access to many of the foods that were available in the east. The first livestock to arrive at the fort were hogs and corn was a staple. The phrase "hogs and hominy" describes many of the pioneers' meals.

A fort was just a temporary stopping place for most settlers. On any given day, a fort would be filled with different kinds of people. Some would be farmers staying just long enough to stake a land claim. Others might be scouts from other settlements or hunters, surveyors, or land speculators just passing through.

Regardless of their reasons for coming, life in the fort and in the surrounding areas required an enormous amount of work. Depending on your age, gender, and time of year, chores my be anything from chopping wood, spinning, weaving, cooking, and hunting to working in the fields, churning, or clearing land. The list of work was nearly endless.

And children were expected to do their share. From the time they were very small, kids were taught to take responsibility and do their part to help the family. It wasn't easy, but hard work was necessary for survival.

HARD TIMES

Unfortunately, Daniel and Rebecca Boone were not strangers to hardship. In 1773, Boone tried to move his family to the Kentucky frontier. James, their oldest son, had stayed behind to gather some much needed supplies with plans of catching up to the group later. Sadly, James and the others in his camp were attacked and tortured by Indians. Only a slave hiding in the bushes survived and informed the rest of the group. As a result, the family turned back and did not move to Kentucky until 1775.

BROOM MAKING

Knife and fork are on display at the Pioneer Museum at Blue Licks Battlefield.

ROAD TO STATEHOOD

NOW THAT'S INTERESTING

- Kentucky's first constitution was written in only eighteen days.

- Kentucky is currently governed by its fourth constitution.

- By 1792, Kentucky's population was around 90,000.

COMMONWEALTH OF KENTUCKY

UNITED WE STAND

DIVIDED WE FALL

STATE SEAL

It is a myth that the woodsman on the state's seal is Daniel Boone. Instead, the two images represent the frontiersman and the statesman—two types of individuals who were important in settling Kentucky.

Constitution Square
Danville, Kentucky

In December 1776, Kentucky officially became Kentucky County, Virginia. However, as Kentucky's population grew, so did the people's desire to form their own state.

On it's tenth **convention** in Danville in 1792, a group of delegates accepted the terms of separation from Virginia. They then drafted Kentucky's constitution. It was accepted on June 1, 1792, and Kentucky officially became the fifteen state of the U.S.

Since then, much has changed about Kentucky. Today, Kentucky's Capitol holds a mural of Daniel Boone looking out over the unsettled land of Kentucky. But, most areas are no longer the wild frontier they once were. Wild game still exists, but not in the number it once was. And, there are no longer bloody battles over land. Instead, we are a modern state filled with people from many different walks of life.

Yet, Kentucky's pioneer spirit remains. Kentuckians are still pioneers in the areas of education, business, medicine, technology, and many other fields. We are still a people exploring, testing, and trying new ideas. Only one question remains... WILL YOU BE A KENTUCKY PIONEER?

Capitol Building
Frankfort, Kentucky

BOONE'S GRAVE

As for Kentucky's most famous frontier hero, Daniel Boone and his family relocated to present-day Missouri in 1799. Poor land claims, taxes, and a growing population forced the great woodsman into another unsettled territory. When he died in 1820, he was buried in a family cemetery next to his beloved Rebecca, who had died seven years earlier.

In 1845, the state of Kentucky wanted to honor its hero and offered to build a monument overlooking Frankfort and the Kentucky River. The remains of both Daniel and Rebecca were moved to the capital city where an impressive funeral was held in Boone's honor. However, there are some who say the bones were switched and are not those of the famous frontiersman. Most Kentuckians proudly disagree, but PERHAPS IT'S A MYSTERY YOU CAN SOLVE!

Glossary

Apprentice— an individual who works for a master to learn a trade.

Convention— a group of people who meet together to deal with a specific issue.

Culture— the way a group of people live and behave; includes music, art, religion, food, clothing, shelter, and other traditions and customs.

Cure— to prepare food in such a way that it will not spoil; may be done through smoking, drying, or salting.

Geographic feature— a distinctive place on the earth's surface such as a valley, mountain, or river; some geographic features can be man-made.

Natural resource— an aspect of nature that allows a person to complete a task or survive (example: fresh water, salt licks, fertile soil, wild game).

Pioneer— any person who is one of the first to explore or settle an area.

Scarce— when there isn't enough of a specific item.

Shelter— a living place that gives protection from the weather.

Wilderness Road— the path created by Daniel Boone and a group of men and followed by thousands of settlers into Kentucky.

Acknowledgments

A book is never the work of a single entity. It is the result of many individuals putting forth their time and talents. A special thank you to the wonderful and generous people at Fort Boonesborough, Fort Harrod, Blue Licks and Constitution Square State Parks. You patiently allowed me to pepper you with seemingly mundane questions. A special thanks to Bill Farmer, whose insights are throughout the book. And, Dr. James Klotter for his editorial insights.

Thank you also to Paula, Michelle, Jo, and Misty at McClanahan Publishing, Inc. Your work is priceless. And, of course, Jim, who quietly toils away, not seeking the spotlight, but whose work is second to none. I will always be grateful.

Of course, a heartfelt thank you goes to my husband, Brad, who, as I'm fond of telling others, "supports my writing habit." What a blessing!

McClanahan Publishing House, Inc. would like to give special thanks to Steve Caudill and the many other reenactors.

Learn more about the pioneers and Kentucky's unique history by visiting some of these historical sites.

Blue Licks Battlefield State Resort Park
Hwy 68
Mount Olivet, KY 41064
http://parks.ky.gov

Boone Station State Historic Site
240 Gentry Road
Lexington, KY 40502
http://parks.ky.gov

Thomas D. Clark Center for Kentucky History
100 West Broadway
Frankfort, KY 40601
http://parks.ky.gov

Constitution Square State Historic Site
134 South Second Street
Danville, KY 40422
http://parks.ky.gov

Cumberland Gap National Historic Park:
South 12th Street, P.O. Box 1848
Middlesboro, KY 40965
www.nps.gov/cuga/

Fort Boonesborough State Historic Park
4375 Boonesborough Road
Richmond, KY 40475
http://parks.ky.gov

Fort Harrod State Park
100 South College Street
Harrodsburg, KY 40330
http://parks.ky.gov